IPHONE X

USER MANUAL

FOR NEWCOMERS

**Complete iOS 12 guide
for beginners and seniors**

Stephen W. Rock

Dedicated to all my readers

Acknowledgement

Ii want to say a very big thank you to Michael Lime, a 3D builder, my colleague. He gave me moral support throughout the process of writing this book.

Table of Contents

Introduction 8

Chapter 1..9

The iPhone X 9

Chapter 2..12

How To Secure Your iPhone With Face ID 12

Setting up Face ID 12

Using the Face ID 13

How To Charge iPhone Wirelessly. 14

Charging wirelessly 14

Chapter 3..16

Tips and tricks for the iPhone X 16

Shoot like a pro 17

Using the app switcher 18

Force the home button back 19

Customize Control Center.............................20

Force apps to close 21

Taking screenshots..22

Force Phone To Reset 23

Shut off alarms with your face. 24

Speedy face ID unlock 25

Access the apple pay easily.....................................26

Specify What Face ID unlocks 27

Enable One-Handed Mode.......................................28

Terminate Face ID Quickly. 29

Easy Control Center Access.....................................30

Make your iPhone X Battery last a decade. 31

Activating Siri 33

Taking Photo In The Portrait Mode..............................34

Using Animoji 35

Use One Tapping To Wake..37

The Beauty Of Slow Sync Flash 38

Chapter 4..39

How To Use Apple Pay 39

Setting Up The Apple Pay...39

Using The Apple Pay..40

Chapter 5..41

Tips for using iOS 12 effectively 41

Saving Your Passwords..42

Ability To Turn On 'Do Not Disturb' During Bedtime....43

Measuring Objects With An App................................44

Insert Siri shortcuts 45

Track your screen time 46

Place Limits on apps...47

Easy Force Closing apps. 48

Chapter 6...49

How To Use Siri On Your Iphone...................................49

How to invoke Siri 49

How to type and ask Siri 51

Tips To Ensure That Siri Serves You Well 52

Chapter 7...55

How To Maintain Your iPhone 55

Chapter 8...59

Prolonging Your iPhones Battery Life. 59

Disclaimer...62

About the author 63

Introduction

The title of this book already gives a hint on what the book is about. It is a guide for new users of the iPhone X.

There are about eight detailed chapters in the book. Dividing the whole book into three parts, the first part introduces you into how to explore the iPhone X, the middle exposes a comprehensive list of tricks and how to execute them, while the last part culminates with useful maintenance tips, including battery and overall iPhone.

Also, with the comprehensive list of commands, you'll definitely learn to be a pro in using Siri, Apple's voice assistant. You'll be a pro in using Apple Pay. You'll be an iOS 12 pro. Yes, an iOS 12 pro.

Now, start savoring the content of this book.

Chapter 1

The iPhone X

On November 3, 2017, Apple launched the iPhone X. And we're totally loving it. Its features are killer.

The iPhone X comes with a dual lens of 12 mp rear camera with a wide angle aperture lens of f/1.8 and f/24 telephoto lens. What more? It also has a front camera of a whooping 7 mega-pixel which enables you to control the exposure or use portrait mode. With its capabilities, you can now experience Augmented Reality (AR). You can use both the TrueDepth or rear camera with AR apps.

Its 7 mp TrueDepth Camera uses face ID and a superb new feature called Animoji. This transmits your facial expression through the camera and to form an animated 3D emoji. The camera is capable of recording over 5o facial muscles movements. When your face is converted to Animoji, you can use it in the messages app.

That's not all. It's all got a 10x Digital zoom, auto flash and an optical zoom. And yes, let's not forget the video capability of the phone. It's got a 4k resolution that allows you to shoot at 60 frames per second. You can also shoot slow-mo at 240 frames per second.

iPhone X also has Hexa Core which provides a better performance with the A11 Bionic chip. Its also got a 64-bit processor that is damn so efficient with a 3GB RAM. And oh yes, it also has an ample storage of up to 64GB or 256GB. No worries about storage space anymore, right?

Now as for Battery, The iPhone X is said to have a 2716 mAh battery and is equipped with wireless charging with accessories that are Qi compatible. Though we are still expecting apple's own AirPower soon.

Regarding the screen size, it's got an OLED display of about 5.8 inches (14.73 cm). With resolution of 2436 x 1125 pixels, the iPhone X is said to be water and dust resistant, which i think is super awesome. Something also worth mentioning is that apple says when looking at the screen from an angle, users may notice a small change in colour.

iPhone X also has apples new Face ID that uses the TrueDepth camera. A look at the camera and the phone engine scans the image, detecting the style and shape of your face to identify it.

Chapter 2

How To Secure Your iPhone With Face ID

Setting up Face ID

Before we set anything up, let's make sure there's nothing blocking your face or the phones TrueDepth camera. Try to keep the phone with arms length. And don't worry about contacts or glasses, Face ID can work with them.

To set it up,
1. Go to **Settings**
2. Choose **Face ID and Passcode**. Enter your passcode.
3. Select **Set up Face ID**
4. Put your phone in front of your face and hit **Get started.**

5. Make sure your face is in the frame. Move your head gently to complete the circle. When it's done, hit **Continue**.
6. You'll be asked to do it a second time. Do the same thing and click **Done**.

Using the Face ID

Tap to wake or raise to wake your phone. Hold it in portrait orientation and it should scan your face.
If you're in bright sunlight, you might want to bring the camera closer to your face.

Face ID has been tested to unlock even when you're wearing sunglasses, but not all. So if you're trying to unlock your phone but it isn't recognizing, pull the sunglass off.

How To Charge iPhone Wirelessly.

Later versions of iPhone (iPhone 8 and higher) have a glass back that enables Qi certified chargers to charge the phone wirelessly. There are many Qi certified chargers. But there are two which are Apple certified; Mophie and Belkin.

Charging wirelessly

To charge wirelessly, what you want to do is;

1. Plug your charger to the power. Be sure to use a power adapter that's recommended by the manufacturer.
2. Make sure to put your charger on a flat surface
3. Lay your iPhone in the middle of the charger with its screen facing upwards and your phone should start charging

That not all. Here are a few things to make to wireless charging run smoothly

- If vibration is turned on, your phone might very well move its position when it gets a notification as you're charging. Try to turn off vibration, at least when you charge
- Make sure your phone isn't connected to a USB when you're charging wirelessly, it won't charge.
- If your iPhone has a thick or magnetic case, remove it before charging. It might charge slowly or not at all.
- When charging, your phone might get somewhat hot. When it does, move it to a cooler environment.

Chapter 3

Tips and tricks for the iPhone X

Shoot like a pro

If there's something we must talk about here, it's the iPhone X ability to shoot videos in high resolution.

And when I say high resolution I mean massive resolution, I mean shooting 4k resolution at 60 frames per second. As with slow motion, it's able to record 1080p at 240 frames per second. Now if you're familiar with the world of video making you'll know that's a lot.

To get to use this awesome feature;
1. Go to **Settings**
2. Choose **Camera**
3. Then **Record video**

You should see a list, choose from what it shows.

To record slow motion, look under **Camera**, a setting called **Record slo-mo** should be there.

Using the app switcher

With the iPhone X, you don't get a home button. Who needs a home button anyway when we've got new features like the app switcher.

Swipe up from the bottom of the screen like you're dong home gesture. But hold at the center of the screen. Form the left side of the screen an indicator should appear. Then you can swipe right or left.

But that kind of a long process and is used to switch to an app that was used a long time ago.

But to move through recent apps quickly, just swipe right to left or left to right from the bottom edge of the screen

Force the home button back

For diehard fans of the home button, there's a way to bring the button back. Okay you know you can't bring possibly bring back the physical home button. But that doesn't mean we are without hope.

We enable the virtual home button. Which really is a piece of cake.
1. Enter settings
2. Choose Accessibility
3. Assistive touch, you can then toggle it on
From here on, you should now see the virtual home button. You can even activate shortcuts by customizing to.

Customize Control Center

Things got way cooler with iPhone X ability to edit what appears in the control center. It really everything lot easier. You can easily reach for stuff without having to travel a long way.

To do this,
1. Enter **Settings**
2. Hit **Control Center**
3. Then **Customize Controls**

From here, you decide what shows up and what doesn't. Like for example, if you're the type that doesn't use much of **flashlight**, you can remove and put something like **Voice memos** that you use regularly.

Force apps to close

There's no home button so you would think that you can't force quit stubborn apps. Actually think again. You can. Though it's a tad more complex than before.

1. Bring the **App Switcher** up. That means swiping up from the bottom corner of the screen
2. **Press** and **hold** the app you want to remove
3. Tap the **red minus** sign at the left corner of the screen.

It's usually believed that forcing apps to quit help to save battery. But actually apple says it does quite the opposite, it reduces the battery.
Some apps are just too stubborn, so when they start acting up, you can follow this method..

Taking screenshots

Are you finding It tricky to take screenshots on your iPhone X? Or do you think screenshots are just for the phone gurus. Trust me, you'll scream when you find out how easy it is to take a screenshot. It's like knife slicing through butter.

Press and hold the **Side Button** and **Volume Up** at the same time. You should hear the shutter sound to signify it's been shot. Try it.

It works right. Told you you'll scream.

Force Phone To Reset

During the course of using your phone there's no way it won't freeze at some point. When that happens, all you just do is reset the phone. What this means is that your phone will shut down and restart again.

To reset;
1. Press the volume up button and release it
2. Press the volume down button and release it
3. Hold the side button down.

After this, it should restart. Then you should see the apple symbol that shows up when the phone is turning on.

Shut off alarms with your face.

Have you ever tried to switch of your blaring alarm in the middle of the night just to find that the touch pad keeps ceasing. Well I know that feeling. It sucks and can be frustrating.

But the iPhone X does away with that problem because you can now shut down alarms with your face. Yup, you don't have to snooze.

Once that alarm starts its daily noise, just bring your phone to your face. Face ID should find your face. Once it finds it, it should please your ears and quiet the volume.

Speedy face ID unlock

If you've been using Face ID, then you know how it works to unlock you phone. You raise it and after Face ID unlocks the phone you swipe up. But do you know that's the slower method.

Yeah you can do it much faster. And it's really easy. All you do is raise and you swipe.

Yes you read right. Just raise and you swipe. The speed and accuracy of Face ID is so top-notch that all you need to do is swipe up as long as the true depth camera is in front of your face. You don't have to wait all year for the lock to open.

Access the apple pay easily

Okay, so now the home button has been discarded. How then do we bring up the apple pay on or phone? Easy. That's what I love about apple. They remove stuffs and replace with way cooler stuffs.

With Apple Pay, all you do is double click the side button on your iPhone X. Then you'll have to verify using Face ID. After verification, you can move on with your transaction.

Specify What Face ID unlocks

Face ID is really beneficial. You don't have to start pressing pins. You just bring the phone to your face and it unlocks the. But the Face ID is not only to unlock the phone. You can also use it to fill forms in Safari, purchase from the app store and verify apple pay.

But all these things could be overwhelming and you may feel weary wary about using Face ID for some stuffs. And there's a way to cancel where you don't want Face ID to function.

1. Go to **Settings**
2. Select **Face ID & Passcode**

From here you can toggle where exactly you want Face ID to work.

Enable One-Handed Mode.

I'm sure you must've taken your time to examine your iPhone X. And as you can see it's no small boy. It's got a very wide screen.

A time might come when you'll have to type singlehandedly. And I tell you that's no easy task. You start you feel pain in your hands and it's just nasty.

But you could say Apple saw this coming. They've provided the one-handed mode. What this does is it compresses the keyboard to be easily accessible by one hand.

To use this feature, hit the **emoji key icon** in the keyboard then choose either left or right handed keyboard and it will swish to a side.

Terminate Face ID Quickly.

If by chance you suddenly start to grow a hatred for the Face ID, you can turn it off. Like for example of you're in a place where you can be forced to look at your phone to unlock it.

As quick as you can, hit the side button five times. It should turn on Face ID immediately. After Face ID is off it will automatically switch to your passcode for you to unlock.

Easy Control Center Access

Reaching from top of your iPhone X top swipe down the control center with one is not exactly the most painless thing to do. But again Apple makes it easier with this setting called Reachability.

To access this;
1. Enter **Setting**
2. Then **General**
3. Select **Accessibility**
4. Then just below **interactions**, turn on **Reachability**

Now that **Reachability** is activated, all you do is swipe down on the **gesture bar** and the screen will move down so that you can be able to touch the top icons.

And it think is better. Less pain more gain.

Make your iPhone X Battery last a decade.

You know that's just an expression right. But there are tricks that you can use to make you go for about a day without needing to charge. In fact depending on how much you use. It can even last you for two days.

First of all, you want to put your phone in **low power mode**.
1. Got to **Settings**
2. Choose **Battery**
3. Then **low power mode**

Next,
1. Enter **Settings**
2. Select **General**
3. Then **Accessibility**
4. Choose **Display accommodations**.
5. Select **Color Filters** and toggle it on
6. Hit **Grayscale**.

Now still in **Display accommodations**,

1. Select **invert colors**
2. Toggle on **classic invert**

Next you want to choose an all-white wallpaper. It will turn to an all-black wallpaper since we've inverted the colors.

Activating Siri

Of course apple has to include Siri in the iPhone X. Siri is the virtual assistant that does what task is given by your voice command. There's a power button at the right side of your iPhone X. Press and hold it to activate Siri.

At the bottom of the screen, you should see the Siri listening sign on the screen. Once you see Siri, you release the button. You can now issue a voice command like "What time is it in Los Angeles?"

Taking Photo In The Portrait Mode.

Using portrait mode on the iPhone X can be very delightful. And you can even use it both on the front camera or the camera at the rear.

Open your camera app. Select portrait. Then you should see an array of Portrait lighting effect options. Like Studio light to brighten the features of the face, Stage light to separate the person in spotlight, Contour light to add directional light and others.

To switch to the front camera, hit the camera rotate icon.

Using Animoji

With the iPhone X you can be able to create an Animoji that mimics your facial expressions and voice and even share it with anyone.

To do this,

1. Open the **messages app** and make as if to start a conversation.
2. Hit the emoji icon
3. Select **Animoji**.
4. Put your face in the frame and start recording
5. You can preview your emoji by click the top corner by the left.
6. To change your Animoji, just choose another Animoji.
7. Choose **send**.

To save an Animoji

1. Open any message that the Animoji is in.
2. Tap and hold the Animoji.
3. Select **save**

Use One Tapping To Wake

I'm sure you know of the other android phones that uses double tap to wake. They've been kinda bragging about this for years now. But the iPhone X has that. In fact I doesn't have that, it has better. A wake feature that needs just one tap.

This feature is ever so nice if you're trying to do quick tasks like looking at notifications without much stress or checking the time. To use this nice feature, just tap any place on the phone's screen.

The Beauty Of Slow Sync Flash

Have you ever taken a picture in the dark? I know I have, using my phones flash as light. And believe me when I say that you wouldn't want to try it again. The image can be really nasty.

But that's because the photo is taken at a high shutter speed. And low lighting and fast shutter speed doesn't work very well together.

But what now happens when the shutter speed is slow or with slow sync flash?. Well I shouldn't say much, try it yourself, you'll be amazed. You'll get a sweet image.

If you want to activate iPhone X slow sync flash, use the flash.

Chapter 4

How To Use Apple Pay

It is now ever easy to use Apple pay. It can even be done through the iMessage app. All you do to activate is place the top of your phone near the **NFC** card terminal while putting your finger on the iPhone's sensor for Touch ID. But to be able to perform all these wonders, you've got set Apple pay up first.

Setting Up The Apple Pay

1. Open **Wallet**
2. Select **Add Credit or Debit card**.
3. Put your card details. Your card will now be verified with your bank
4. Once that is done, you are able to use Apple Pay.

Using The Apple Pay.

1. Put your phone near the card reader and what will appear on the screen should be the image of your card.
2. If you use Touch ID, Place your finger on the Touch ID sensor. Once your fingerprint is confirmed, you're golden.

If you want another card, press the one that is on the screen and select a different card. Real simple, uh?

However if your phone uses Face ID like iPhone X and higher, the process is a little different. It's not hard though. You just click twice on the side button. Then put your face to the camera so it can scan your face. After this, you simply hold the phone toward the card reader. Double click the side button again, if you want to use another card and just select a different card.

Chapter 5

Tips for using iOS 12 effectively

Saving Your Passwords

In the iOS 12 there a totally cool feature that helps users be able to follow up on their passwords. The new iOS is armed with a feature called **AutoFill Passwords**. This is usually kept in the iCloud keychain.

With this, you can add your own username and passwords from your **Settings app** to set for only some apps and websites. This feature will fill in your information automatically for you once you use Face ID or Touch ID after it identifies the ones that are logged

Ability To Turn On 'Do Not Disturb' During Bedtime.

The **Do Not Disturb** option got totally revamped in the iOS 12. With its extra feature, you are able to customize it more to suit your taste. Not only can you state clearly what times you want **Do Not Disturb** to be on at day, you can even set it to Bedtime mode.

If you set it, this will quiet down all the notifications all the way till the morning. To let you know that it the feature is set, the screen will display just the date and time and become dim.

Measuring Objects With An App.

Using the camera of your iPhone, iOS 12 allows you to measure objects with AR. When you use the measure app, you'll be able to measure different objects.

All you do is,

1. Open the **Measure app**.
2. Fix your iPhone's camera on the object to measure
3. Follow the guides it gives to line up your phone correctly.
4. Next, to view the measurements, you just click the display

Every display will always show the option to switch form inches to centimeters. Of course it doesn't give an accurate measurement like a hardware tape rule, it is really handy if you just want to take a quick measurement of an item.

Insert Siri shortcuts

There's a new advancement with Siri in the iOS 12. It's the option to add immediate actions and shortcut to Siri. Thought this option is still in beta for now and you can't do plenty with it, there are still some perks you can enjoy.

Like how you can set a voice commands so that Siri can do some specific tasks. Example, **View New photos.**

If you want to set a voice command'

1. Enter your **Settings**.
2. Selects **Siri and Search**
3. Click **My Shortcuts**

Once that is open you will be able select anyone that Siri suggests.

Track your screen time

In the iOS 12, apple is trying to urge us to use our phones lesser so we can have time for other important activities. There's this new feature, **Screen time**.

Screen time is a opportunity for you to set Downtime, check your phone usage and find out which apps are really eating away your time. When you use down time, you are able to put away your phone by restraining some applications from forwarding notifications.

Place Limits on apps

This is also one of the perks of screen time. It enables you to set app limits. This will enable you to reduce the time you spend on certain apps. You will be able to set how long the ban should last and for which days.

If you want to set app limits.

1. Fire up the **Settings app**
2. Move to **Screen time**
3. Then **App limits**. Select the groups of apps you want to set limit. Click the **Add**

Easy Force Closing apps.

With the iOS 12, the process of force closing apps is a lot simpler. Not only simpler also quicker. All you do is swipe up from the bottom of the display and just start swiping the apps you want to quit like that.

Y'know, previously force closing apps on phones without home button on previous iOS will have to take a longer method. You'll have to swipe up and hold down and wait before a minus sign will appear, then you now click

But now with newer phones like the iPhone XS and XS Max, they all have the iOS 12, so the process is a lot simpler.

Chapter 6

How To Use Siri On Your Iphone

Siri is the ever helpful apple voice assistant that you dish out commands to on your iPhone and it just it just carries it out for you.

But something to note is that there's not a specific app icon for Siri that you just tap and it open. So how then do you access Siri. For newer generations of iPhones, accessing Siri can be a little confusing even if you have been using previous versions of iPhone. All of that we will cover here

How to invoke Siri

By Clicking the home button or side button

On older versions of iPhone, pressing and holing the home button on your device will call up Siri. But on the iPhone X and higher, you summon Siri by pressing the button at the side of the phone.

By using the Bluetooth headset button.

If you use a headset that has remote, press and hold the button at the center and you should hear a ding.

By saying hey Siri

If your iPhone is iOS 8 or higher, you can summon Siri hands free by saying 'Hey Siri'. But you've got to first set it up.

1. Got to **Settings**
2. Choose **Siri & Search**
3. Enable **Listen For** 'Hey Siri' and obey the prompts it provides
4. From now you can summon Siri without having to press anything just say **"Hey Siri"**

What Can Siri do for you,

- Send messages for you
- Set a timer for you
- Play music
- Send tweets
- Check the weather
- Schedule events

- Send emails
- Calculate
- Find locations

Here are some things you can ask Siri

- 'Hey Siri, Set an alarm for 6 am'
- 'Hey Siri, What is the time New York?'
- 'Hey Siri, schedule a meeting with Sarah for Tuesday at 11oclock
- 'Hey Siri, how cold will it be today?'
- 'Hey Siri, remind me to do the dishes?'
- 'Hey Siri, play me Roar by Katy Perry'
- 'Hey Siri, call David Randall
- 'Hey Siri, open the Settings App'
- 'Hey Siri, how do I say hello in Spanish?'
- 'Hey Siri, who is the President of Iceland?'
- 'Hey Siri, turn off Bluetooth'

How to type and ask Siri

If you're the type that doesn't really fancy talking to Siri, you don't have to say something. You can just type your command. Though you'll have to set it up first

Here's how.

1. Enter **Settings**
2. Go to **General**
3. Select **Accessibility**
4. Move down to Siri and click the line
5. Switch on **Type To Siri**
6. The next time you activate Siri, all you do is type in your command

Tips To Ensure That Siri Serves You Well

While the apples virtual assistant is known for its top notch abilities, you may encounter some problems with it. Implement these few tips to allow Siri to better

Control how long Siri will listen

You have the power to control how long Siri will continue to encode your commands. You don't have to wait for it to recognize that you have stopped talking.

Just make sure that while you're asking your question or saying your command, you're holding down the power button

Alter Siri's language.

One of the key reasons why Siri may not understand your commands well can be because of your language. Even in English. Let's say you speak UK English. Siri may misinterpret your commands. So what you want to do is set the English to 'English (United Kingdom)

To adjust the language,
1. Enter the **Settings**
2. Go to **Siri and Search**
3. Select Language
4. Choose your desired language.

Having Smooth Data Connection

If you don't have data connection, Siri won't work. How Siri functions is that it records your voice and sends it to a server which converts your sayings and gives it back as text.

So if you're not connected to the internet, Siri is not going to work.

Changing Siri's gender

If you're a male and you prefer to have a male virtual brother around, you can switch the gender. Same goes for females.

Just,

1. Enter **Settings**
2. Then **Siri and Search**
3. Choose **Siri Voice**
4. Select your preferred voice.

Chapter 7

How To Maintain Your iPhone

We all know that iPhones are not biscuit change. They cost high. Well, they give superb quality so they are very well worth it. But such an investment will go to total waste if you don't take proper care of your treasure.

So here are some iOS maintenance tips for your consumption.

Put The Unwanted In The Garbage Truck

Do you remember that game that your buddy told you to try out and you felt it was total trash? Or yes, that app your neighbor introduced to you only for to find that it was a complete waste of time. Yes those applications.

I'm pretty sure they are still sitting there in you app list

Throw them out and send them packing immediately. Not only do they use up the space of the phone, they also make it sluggish and your device slow. To delete an app, press and hold the app until it shakes like it's waving 'hey look at me' and delete or press the X at the corner.

Back Them Up

It's funny how many people do the bad stuff and only few do the good, like backing up your iPhones. You need to train yourself so that it becomes a habit.

Reason why backing up is so essential is because of this. Let's say your iPhone gets missing (I really hope that doesn't happen) or you there was a software update gone wrong or your device becomes faulty, retrieving your files will be almost impossible.

So don't wait for me, just back your phone up. You can back your phone up with iCloud or iTunes. In fact what's stopping you, just do both

Update iOS

You be like 'Who needs an update. My iOS is just fine'. And I want you discard that feeling and throw it far away.

You need an update. With every new iOS there are fixes to bugs, updates for security, and brand new features and perks. You stick to your old iOS and it will be like you're living in the Stone Age.

What more, updating is like the easiest thing to do. Since we have OTA (Over The Air), updating iOS is just a matter of minutes.

To update,
1. Make sure to back up your phone as we warned earlier
2. Enter **Settings**

3. Then **General**
4. Then Choose **Software update**.
5. If an update is available, click **Download and install**.

Phone case and Screen protector

We all know how phone cases and screen protectors saves our lives every once in a while. Okay, not our life per say, it's our phones. Whenever your phone drops, a protective phone case will help to absorb the effect and shock of the fall.

And screens, oh screens are really special. And believe me when I say that you do not want them to break. So just buy a screen protector.

When you're purchasing either of the two, make sure it's of good quality and the design is what you desire.

Chapter 8

Prolonging Your iPhones Battery Life.

As with maintenance of phones, we all know how much battery means to us. Check out these tips to extend your phones battery life.

Forget Quitting Apps

You may probably be doing this, quitting apps regularly, I usually do so too in the past. But stop. you might think that you're saving you're battery, but actually you're degrading it.

In 2014, Apple explained to us that quitting apps sucks more battery as the next time you want to open the app, it will start all over again thereby, eating the batter.

Using The Auto Brightness Option.

Using full screen brightness sucks away your battery and I'm sure you know that. Unless you really need the extra brightness, don't be stubborn just use auto brightness.

This adjusts the screens brightness to the surroundings you're in.

Turn Low Power Mode On

Normally when you're phone reaches 20%, you'll be prompted to switch to low power mode. But you don't have to wait for your phone to urge you before you switch it. You can do it right after you finishing charging.

Low power mode stops all the background tasks and gives you more battery.

Turn Off Bluetooth.

It's not a new thing that putting your Bluetooth on regularly reduces the battery life. So if you're not using the Bluetooth, just put it off

Disclaimer

In as much as the author believes beginners will find this book helpful in learning how to use the iPhone X, it is only a small book. It should not be relied upon solely for all iPhone tricks and troubleshooting.

About the author

Stephen Rock has been a certified apps developer and tech researcher for more than 12 years. Some of his 'how to' guides have appeared in a handful of international journals and tech blogs. He loves rabbits.

Facebook page @ Techgist